girls trapped in dreams

hazel folsom

Girls Trapped in Dreams
Copyright © 2021 by Hazel Folsom
All rights reserved. No part of this book may be reproduced or used in any manner without the prior written permission of the copyright owner, except for the use of brief quotations in a book review.

Paperback ISBN: 9798700319836
Ebook ASIN: B08W8GZV3L

Printed by kindle direct publishing in the United States of America.

First Edition

dedication

oh little girl alone in your room
you are not alone in the world

daydreams

recipe for cake

poems written for emily
I hope she likes blank verse.
I hope she likes the cakes I bake
I'm not sure which is worse:
that which is sickly sweet
or that which is sweet sour?
I hope she likes the words I write
I hope she likes the flour.

girls with twigs in their hair

take me along on your wild ride
through your world of fantasy

let me join you in your wild song
I'll howl along as you sing

for girls should be feral and wild
should run as if still a child
should be given no limitations
in this universe of their creation.

complements

butterflies and bumblebees
wishing wells and willow trees
queen of hearts and jacks of trade
all the plans that we have made.
there's so much for us to do
me and you?
me and you.

the archaeologist

under the earth
lived a pile of bones
they once were connected
before they became stone

where did they travel
what things do they know?
do I uncover their secrets
or leave them alone?

the scientist

I think I would like
to keep my heart in a jar
to watch the way it beats

I'd observe its pulse
and take note of its tone
and measure the size of its strength

I would like to understand
such a strange specimen
but I'm not sure I ever could

I'll keep it in a jar
for when it drops
the glass breaks first

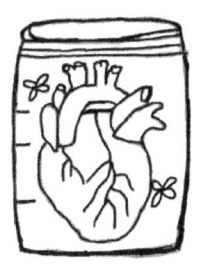

<u>*portrait of the artist*</u>

if my words were a portrait of you
the curve of the letters
could not do justice to the beauty
of your smile, of your eyes
that reach into my soul and
take hold of my heart that
I've kept beating for you,
beating for the thought of you,
beating for the dream of
you and me together,
not only on a page but
in a home, in a world,
that is filled with our love
but cannot contain it, for its greatness
reaches beyond its ends
past this life and into another
this love
which can neither die
or end or break or finish
but continues like a song
beating on and on and on and on and on and on
forever.

love of the artist

she is a painter of words
a sculptor of mood into verse
her page is a canvas covered in her thoughts
in her wondrous imagination
that I cannot begin to explain

capsule

I hold my dreams in my stomach
in the expanding part of me
in the dissolving acidity
that breaks apart my fears

I hold my dreams in my head
in the hardest part of me
amongst my biggest mockeries
that tell me all my flaws

I hold my dreams in my hands
in the busy part of me
which bring to life creativity
that illustrate my faith

I hold my dreams inside of me
but they are ever growing
from out of me they will spill out
and still do not stop flowing.

food for worms

the trunk of his body
the branches his veins
leaves fall from his fingers
his hair brings the rain
mushrooms spring from out of his mind
he does not mourn
for what's left behind
the roots, through his sneakers,
dig into the earth
he is decomposing
to give life new birth.

a gift

I guess that is the price of the sun
its kiss is a burn
your skin comes undone
it peels away like a cocoon
to bare your soul
to something new

eclipse

if I could breathe in the sun
I'd take the light into my lungs
I'd keep its warmth within my heart
and just for you I would impart
a note of its golden melody
a drop of celestial sherry
and breathe that sol into your lips
my beloved, darling eclipse

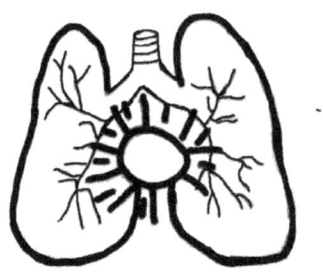

memories

foundation

what a great foundation is a structure like a writing desk
to be raised on words, on goosebumps from dreams
that play in my mind, that raised me in my imagination.

from then to now

I used to be a dancer,
well – alone in my room
I'd do awful pirouettes and make my arms move

I used to be an explorer
with my little red wagon
my hound dog beside me, we fought off the dragons

I used to be a musician
I'd sing to the trees
they cheered me on loudly and shook all their leaves

encore! encore! please, carry on!
and all these years later
I hum that faded song

I dance in the kitchen
I sing to my cat
I explore the pages of the internet

they say, girl, you've grown up
you can't dream forever
give fantasy up
pull yourself together

but I can't let go of what I know in my heart
gives me a purpose
and inspires my art

some of these dreams
may never come to fruition
but I am not me
without my ambition

gus & george

the things that we schemed
back when were girls
who had room to dream
and the craziest curls

sock drawer

you found in my sock drawer a pile of rocks
some dried leaves and roses
an old music box
a birthday card I got in 2015
used movie tickets
and grocery receipts
a matchstick that's been lit (I should throw that out)
and lots of other things
you don't know about
a cheap deck of cards, its aces all missing
multiple bookmarks and something
that's hissing??
a guitar pick
some buttons
a stick!
and among my collection,
   there are no socks.

the watermelon

the watermelon was large and green
it fell from his hands, it was so slippery
it hit the ground and opened with a crack
so I sat beside it in the garden, by the ants
I scooped out the pink pieces with my little hands
and I sat there for hours, it took great patience
I think to this day, it's my greatest accomplishment
the day I ate a watermelon all by myself

hide & seek

hiding between the branches
of the large pine tree
I laughed as my mom pretended
she couldn't find me.
I giggled as she called my name
and much to my delight
she wandered about looking until
she found me and held me tight.

martha jane

you walked here first
upon this ground
long before
there was a town
when there were fields
without structures
and you loved the land
and you loved these wonders
you traveled far
I've traveled too
and I did not know
I was so close to you
now here I am
in this same place
it feels to me
that this was fate
to stand here
before your grave
grateful for all
that you once gave

amelia

it's too dangerous
it's never been done
what makes you think
you will be the one
to defy what others
have long thought impossible?
before you can start
they'll paint you your struggle.

I'm so defiant
I can't tell you why
I'll take all their warnings
with me to the sky

do not tell me how far I can fly.

mary

you left your homeland on a ship
you sailed across on hope

the ocean surrounded you
like your mother's hug goodbye
you fought your fear
for what you believed could be
lead on by faith

the skyline was growing
a comet passed through the sky,
a cross clasped in your hand
you carried traditions
in your suitcase

you came to america
you didn't stop dreaming

h

we walked through the grocery store
so you could pick out a birthday card
I laughed with you while we husked corn
and you cheated while playing cards

my voicemail box is always full
with messages that you left me
and I wish I'd answered your call
instead of letting the phone ring

I have a box of your old things
some old pieces of jewelry
the virgin mary on a pin
and other things you shared with me

I still feel little,
you were so great
I hope someday I'll
have your same strong faith.

lightning bugs and lightning bolts

when I was little, I spent my summers chasing lightning bugs.
I can remember the feel of the grass on my legs
the humidity from the day still on my cheeks.
I chased their little lights flashing in the dark
trying to anticipate where they'd go next.
I'd capture fireflies and put them in some kind of mason jar
to give me comfort as I fell asleep
and to let them go free in the morning.

when I was little, I started watching thunder storms
from under the cover of my front porch
with my hound dog beside me.
she was terrified and so was I
but I had to be brave for her
so, I'd sit in the dark in the storm and watch for the light
and ever since then I've felt luck is a bolt of lightning.

thinking back on it now, I feel like these two things were
preparing me for life.
I think they taught me to love things that are temporary,
that goodness is often here and then gone,
that in the darkness, there are flashes of light.

bedtime stories

an evening with the tricksters

I dreamed that I would runaway
to live my life with wild fae.
we dance through the courts
from night until day.
and amongst the pixies,
the goblins, the sprites,
I found myself a lovely knight.
an offered chalice
I had to decline
for everyone knows
not to drink faerie wine.
let it pass your lips
and forever you'll stay
in the world with the wild fae.

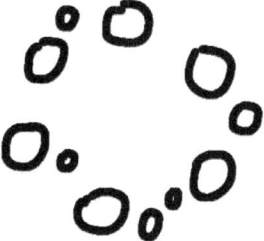

prince charming

once upon a time
a princess sat in her tower
a prince came to save her
but he was soon devoured.

gretel's mistake

little witch shoved in her oven
is greatly missed by her coven.
they vow to avenge the death of their sister
and look to find the one who killed her.

little gretel in the candy cottage
falls asleep with the knowledge
that the witch who caught her is dead,
not knowing what nightmares yet lay ahead.

this here was gretel's mistake
she never considered she'd meet the same fate.
for all of you who do read this story
and do not want their own end to be so gory,
it would do you well to learn this verse:
if you burn a witch,
you face a curse.

angel

angel at her harp
she plays a pious melody
her faith seems like fantasy

oh how she makes me want to believe

face to the sun

girls without wings
reach up to the sun
friends with the breeze
their braids come undone

falling like feathers
driven by lust
how does it feel
to be icarus?

<u>webs we weave</u>

spinning a story out of the lies of my heart
my heart, that ancient storyteller
that Arachne had no time to unravel

<u>daughter of zeus</u>

I am zeus's daughter
whether I like it or not.
we both have a temper
you could say our heads are hot.

we are both leaders,
though sometimes self-proclaimed.
if he'd give me his lightning
I'd challenge his fame.

<u>*circe and odysseus*</u>

she watched him as he sailed away
she always knew he would not stay
he had a kingdom
she would never know
for from her island
she could not go.
do you think he broke her heart
when from her he did depart?

gorgon

monster in her cave
brings all men to stony graves.
her many eyes look out to the sea
and try to block the memory -
in the temple poseidon was cruel
he used medusa like a tool.
when caught, he left her distressing
but his poor victim was given a blessing.

many others would call it a curse
but where men are bad, the gods are worse.
still some do not understand
that kindness moved athena's hand.
this is not the saddest end
her snakes are not her only friends.

zeus and athena

athena sprang from zeus's head
"she is my creation," the boastful god said.
but she was born with wisdom her own
he cannot take credit for all that she's known.
I think the same can be said of all fathers,
they pale in comparison to their beautiful daughters.

persephone dreams

    tricked into eating
    six seeds from the pomegranate
    five took the sunlight
    four took the planet
    three took her mother she would leave behind
    two took the flowers
    one took the vines

now in Hades she does not always stay.
what do you think she dreams while she is away?

    one for seasons end
    two to meet the grim
    three for the river styx
    four to be back with him
    five she longs to be there on her throne
    six bites gave the queen of death
    her underworld home.

nightmares

<u>*daisy*</u>

and he called you a dream
and you knew it was a lie.

you remember it like a shock
like it happened yesterday
like it happened years ago
like you wish you didn't remember it at all
and sometimes you can still hear it
ringing in your ears
you can still remember what they said
but you can't recall the words
this wasn't supposed to happen
at times you still feel scared
and it plays in your head
it takes up your whole world.

<u>*then there was smoke*</u>

you were a fire
and I didn't give you room to breathe.

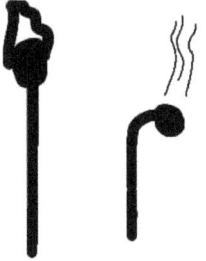

panicking

panic
at losing you
sickness
at the very thought of growing apart from you
weeping
for joy should I find you again
screeching
when I cannot tell where dreams end

wait it out

pulse racing,
anxiety overtaking,
no way to hide the fact that
I am shaking.
can't clear my head

although I try
taking breaths
too many, too quickly
again I try
counting shapes
killing time.

effigies

he watches me with marble eyes
the kind I think could hypnotize.
do you not know how it feels
to love someone that's not alive?

routine

are we not robots,
repeating the same monotonous brain numbing tasks
every day
going through the motions of every day chores
pushing back our every life dreams?

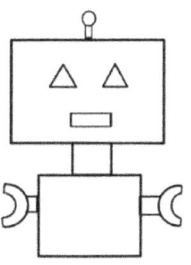

are u mad at me?

I think I've disappointed emily
she hasn't talked to me for weeks
I haven't seen her around
and I'm dying to hear her speak

it feels like I'm regressing
and it's awfully depressing
to feel you cannot do your best
without another's blessing

old friends

and so they drifted apart
until they were entirely separate constellations.

<u>nostalgia</u>

to beg for trees
for childhood dreams
for a time when peace
seemed worth keeping
before the nightmares that came
when I was not sleeping.

space

you say were on different wavelengths
I never thought I would need a new ocean

3:00 a.m.

liberté

at night there are no rules to break
there are no rules to break but one
defy the night, remain awake
breathe free until the rising sun

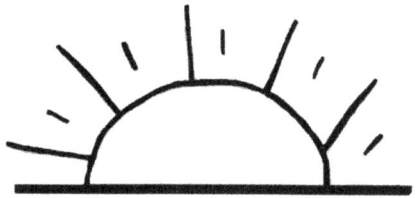

salutations

even though you are far from me
more than I wish you were
i can't help but hope you are happy,
loving and secure. signed,
your friend

night drives

in the middle of nowhere again
the open road ahead of us
the radio glows as it hums.
the glass is cool like ice.
the stars up above are a puzzle
I try to match them up
this moment could be an hour
this hour may never stop.
this is when I feel most at peace
when I feel most together.
the road goes on and on and on
I hope it last forever.

goosebumps

the best kind of goosebumps
are the ones I get when I write
under the light of the moon.

the best kind of heartbeats
are the ones that sound
when you enter the room.

<u>*moonlight*</u>

the little plants in my room
reach up toward the moon
and mimic my cry
for things gone too soon
for petals that wilt
and snowfall that melts
for childhood dreams
and peace I once felt

expectations

as women we are expected
to do things kindly

as heroes we are meant
to face fear bravely

as children we are allowed
to dream limitlessly

as writers we are asked
to write truthfully

the door

the door
stands between me
and every damned thing
that traps me
and demands of me
many things
which I am not yet ready
to give.

speak

you will never have to bow to me
like you bowed your head in murmured whispers
of what you wished you had said
out loud.

fin

girls trapped in dreams
they live in their heads
building up worlds
while safe in their beds.

girls trapped in space
amongst venus and saturn
collect the stars
and lay them in patterns.

girls trapped in words
just like me
are busy escaping
reality.

girls who are trapped
we all want one thing,
all that we wish is
to be *free*.

Acknowledgments

    I want to thank everyone who has supported me and this book. To the community that raised me and friends online that I have never met in real life. I can't think of a time when I have felt so loved by such a large and great group of people. It is truly overwhelming.

    I would most like to thank my Aunt Bea, who inspired my love for reading. I will always be so grateful for you and the poems and dreams you shared with me.

    To my parents and brothers who treat me like a queen. To my grandmothers who taught me to love reading and art and my grandfathers who planted in me a desire to help others.

    To my aunts, uncles, and cousins who are great examples. To my little cousins - don't grow up quite yet.

    To Grace, who has been an incredible editor, supporter, and friend. And to Laramie and Tanna who have listened to a million rants at all hours of the night, even if they were exhausted.

    To Cassie and the Petersons who might as well be family.

    And to all other friends who dreamt by my side, even if it was for a short time.

Last, but not least, to anyone who reads this, I sincerely hope you were able to find something in these words. It is scary to share these thoughts with the world, but I did in the hopes that someone who needs it will find it.

In literature, I have found great comfort, understanding, escape, and motivation. I have often felt like I was alone in this world, stuck in my own mind. I'm grateful for the books and authors that taught me this wasn't the case.

If you are the same, please know that you are not alone. I hope you can continue to dream.

About the Author

Hazel Folsom studied Communication: Public Relations and English at Brigham Young University Idaho. She currently claims Idaho as her home. She loves music, reading, traveling, and her dogs.
Girls Trapped in Dreams is her first book.

You can find her online @hazelwrote
her website: hazelfolsom.carrd.co

Made in the USA
Middletown, DE
28 February 2021